ZD3, the Handy Robot

By Joy Cowley

Illustrated by Joe L. Lai and Alan Wang

DOMINIE PRESS

Pearson Learning Group

Paperback ISBN 0-7685-1082-1
Printed in Singapore
4 5 6 7 8   09 08 07 06 05

Dominie
Press

Pearson Learning Group

1-800-321-3106
www.pearsonlearning.com

Table of Contents

Chapter One
No Ordinary Robot

Cherry Pie Elementary
was no ordinary school.
Its janitor was a robot,
and not an ordinary robot, either.
ZD3 was a happy and helpful robot,
and she had a tin dog called K9.

Mr. Pit, the librarian
at Cherry Pie Elementary,
needed new bookshelves
for the library.
"Please help me, Miss ZD3," he said.

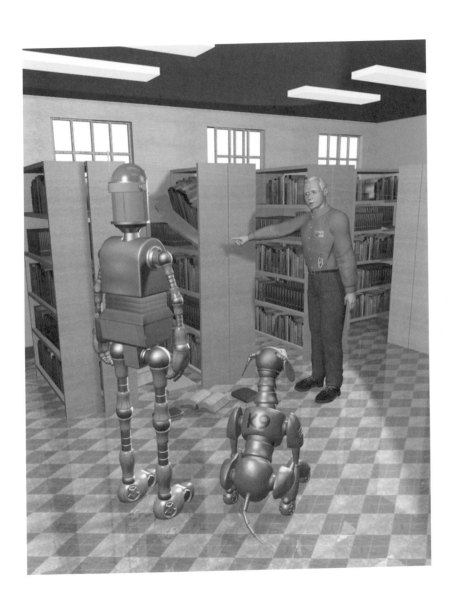

ZD3 replied, "Mr. Pit, do not fear.
New bookshelves will soon be here.
K9, be a good dog
and bring me my fixing bag."

Robot dog K9 went *yip, yip, yip,*
which meant *yes, yes, yes,*
and away he went
to fetch the fixing bag.

ZD3 brought in some lumber
from the school shed.

She sang a happy working song.

Oh give me a home
where the asteroids roam.
Where the moon ships
and space shuttles play.

Where never is heard
the tweet of a bird
and you don't know
if it's nighttime or day.

Chapter Two

New Bookshelves

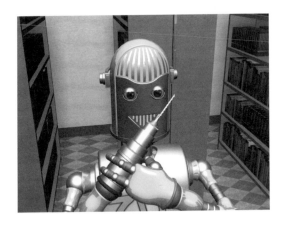

ZD3 opened her fixing bag.
She took out a saw and a drill.
She unscrewed her right hand,
put it down on the carpet,
and then screwed the saw
onto her wrist.

Her powerful batteries
made the saw go fast.
Wah, wah, wah!

Sawdust flew into the air
as she cut shelves from the lumber.
Wah, wah, wah!

K9, who also liked to be helpful,
ran around with a vacuum cleaner
to get rid of the sawdust.
Wah, wah, wah!

Soon all the shelves were cut.
ZD3 unscrewed the saw,
put it back in her fixing bag,
and screwed a drill onto her wrist.
Bzz-bzz. Bzz-bzz.

With K9's help, she put screws
in the shelves to hold them together.
Her drill hand worked quickly.
Bzz-bzz. Bzz-bzz.

"All finished, Mr. Pit," she said.
"Two new sets of bookshelves."

"Wonderful!" cried the happy Mr. Pit.
"Thank you, Miss ZD3!"

"You are very welcome," said ZD3.
"I will help you put the books away."

She took the drill off her wrist
and looked on the carpet.
"Now where did I put my right hand?"

She looked in her fixing bag.
"K9, have you seen my right hand?"

K9 shook his head
and went *yap, yap, yap,*
which meant *no, no, no.*

Chapter Three

Very Attached to It

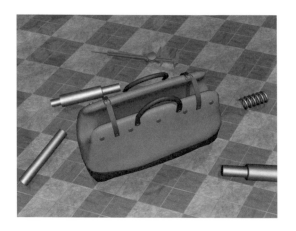

Mr. Pit and K9 helped ZD3
look for her missing hand.
They took everything
out of the fixing bag.
They went over every bit of the carpet.

They looked in and on and behind
all the books.
They found a green pen,
a pack of bubble gum,
and a toy astronaut, but no hand.

Mr. Pit sighed.
"What a pity to lose
such a useful hand."

"I was very attached to it,"
said ZD3. She looked at K9.
"Are you sure you don't have it?"

Yap, yap, yap, barked K9.

"Does your hand have batteries?"
asked Mr. Pit. "Could it have walked
away on its fingers?"

ZD3 shook her head.

"Well," said Mr. Pit,
"you'll just have to go to town
and buy another one."

"Where?" asked ZD3.

"From the secondhand shop,"
said Mr. Pit. "Ha ha ha.
That was a joke."

"I see," said ZD3,
but she didn't laugh.

Chapter Four

Hunt

Soon everyone at Cherry Pie
Elementary School
knew about ZD3's missing hand.
All the children and teachers
had a robot hand hunt
in the school and the schoolyard.

They found an empty bird's nest,
a missing soccer ball,
and the principal's lunch,
but they didn't find anything
that looked like a robot's hand.

That afternoon, a first grade class
made a hand from gold paper.
It had long, red fingernails
and two rings with sparkly stones.

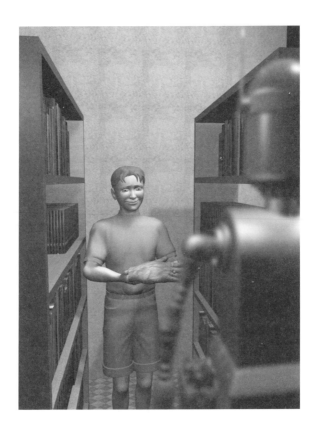

"It's very beautiful," said ZD3.

"You can stick it on with tape,"
said a boy called Brandon,
"but don't get it wet."

"Thank you," said ZD3.
"I'll remember that."

She put the paper hand
in her fixing bag.
"I wish I could find my own hand,"
she said sadly.

"It's a mystery, that's what it is,"
said Mr. Pit, scratching his head.

Chapter Five

It Looks Like A Hand

Miss Crust, the principal,
brought ZD3 a hand
made from a rubber glove
stuffed with cotton wool.

"As you can see, Miss ZD3,
this isn't very grand,
but it looks like a hand
and you can get the rubber wet,"
said Miss Crust.

"You are very kind," said ZD3,
putting the rubber hand
in her fixing bag.

Miss Crust said,
"We'll put a LOST notice
on the school bulletin board.
Whoever finds your real hand
will get a five-dollar reward."

"Thank you," said ZD3.

After Miss Crust had gone,
ZD3 said to her little tin dog,
"If I were not a robot,
I would weep big tears."

K9 understood.
If he were not a robot,
he would have licked ZD3's
one good hand.

Chapter Six

Oh, Goodness Yap!

There was a notice
on the wall beside the office.

LOST:
$5.00 reward for the return
of a right robot hand,
four fingers and a thumb,
made of silver metal
with a screw joint at the wrist.
Contact Miss Crust, Principal,
Cherry Pie Elementary School.

"That'll do the trick,"
Miss Crust told ZD3.

But Mr. Pit, the librarian,
was sure the hand hadn't been lost.
"Someone took it," he said.

"But who?" asked ZD3.
"There was only me and you
and K9 in the library."

Mr. Pit whispered,
"Are you sure your dog
didn't take it away
and bury it like a bone?"

ZD3 shook her head.
"K9 is a robot dog.
Robot dogs don't eat,
and they don't bury bones.
Besides, that hand
doesn't have a single bone in it."
Yip, yip, yip!
K9 wagged his tin tail
and leaned against ZD3.

Then K9 remembered something.

Oh, *yap!* Oh, *yap!* Oh, goodness *yap!*

His tail stopped wagging.
His ears drooped.

"What is it, K9?" said ZD3.

K9 ran to the library closet
and dragged out the vacuum cleaner.

"Tell him to put that back,"
said Mr. Pit. "Can't he see
that the carpet's clean?"
Yap, yap, yap, barked K9,
his tin paws scratching
at the vacuum cleaner.

"Wait a minute!" cried ZD3,
opening the machine.
Suddenly, she saw five fingers
and one thumb
poking up through sawdust.

"My hand!" she cried.
"My wonderful, useful hand!"

Mr. Pit stared at the hand.
"Your dog sucked it up
in the vacuum cleaner!
That wasn't very smart."

"But it was very smart of him
to remember where it was,"
said ZD3, brushing the sawdust
off her beautiful right hand.
Clunk! She screwed it onto her wrist.